cover photo by Salvador Martin Yeste on Unsplash

The Beach
and other poems
by Elliot M. Rubin

Dedication
To my grandchildren
Shane, Isabelle, Jonathan, Carter,
Alexandra, Melanie, Mollie, and Madison

In memory of my father
Herman S. Rubin
who wrote poetry all his life

preface
I believe poetry is to be read and understood by all. It needs to be written in plain language for everyone's enjoyment.

Too often, poets write in-depth, penetrating poems where you need to be well-read and/or versed in literature nuances to appreciate the poetry, not this book or any of my writings. I try to write so everyone can enjoy a few moments of intellectual satisfaction without consulting a dictionary or encyclopedia.

Table of Contents

sabbath question

as i walk by the worship building
on the town square
tower bells ring out,
i look to see if god's angels
are outside
waving me in
to meet,
to talk to,
to see
if i have anything of value to say

does god want to hear my trivia
while there are so many
other worthwhile things
as i watch the sinners walk-in
every week
            never reforming?

why bother her/him/them on the one day of rest?

street justice

theaters let out,
sidewalks in manhattan crowded,
people to walk in the street
dodging cars who race
to beat red lights on cross avenues–
dressed in suits, they stare at a dumpster
by the curb filled with trash
from a closed restaurant,
while a homeless man
digs through looking for food–
elongated limousines parked
in no parking areas
wait for riders, one of which has his back
to a building wall
as a thug presses a knife against his chest,
while hundreds of people walk by
ignoring the felony, looking
at the long limo waiting down the block
while its passenger hands over valuables,
or the guy picking through the dumpster–
the victim afterward runs down the block
to his waiting ride,
while the thief turns to run across the street
as a speeding car from eight avenue hits him

after she left

he sits on the lumpy upholstered chair
scavenged from the streets
in a sparse one-room apartment;
opens a can of beer,
lights a cigarette

he exhales remnants
of his caffeine addiction,
watches gray smoke
dance in the air
from the night's street light
as it streams in the window
under yellowed shades

wishes he could move
as gracefully
as the smoke, once more

at seventy-five
alone in the world
depressed
realizes he screwed up his life;
the best he can do
is rent a wife for an hour or so,
then wait for sunrise

youthful memories of havana

he can feel cuba in his bones
while standing next to her
at the point in key west,
looking over
crashing caribbean waves–
in the distance
sailboats with arms outstretched,
full of bright white canvas
catch the wind while she
paints a picture in his head,
as she holds his hand
to tell him
of sweet havana nights
from her youth

he eagerly waits till evening
to be in her arms
as she wraps her mind
around memories
still alive in her heart;
sharing her intimacy with him
as she did with her first lover
back in vedado, havana

movies in her mind

in her cross-wired mind
life is a black and white movie
filled with shades of gray,
sparking whitest whites of joy,
darkest black of depression,
ending with credits
of her doctor
signing
a death certificate

in reality
she leads a technicolor life
filled with reddest rubies,
whitest diamonds,
enormous mansion,
and chauffeur-driven limos—
on occasion, when her mind
lets her leave the bed,
she puts on a smile,
then shows up for life

costco 7:15 pm wednesday night

after years of doing this
store staff call them the bookclub–
a buck fifty for a hot dog and drink
the seniors meet every wednesday
in the evening
to munch, talk, then shop–
they sit till closing
when the gates go down
at eight-thirty, the
afternoon crew leaves,
cleanup starts in the aisles;
then the manager,
at nine o'clock asks them to go–
they stand outside continue to talk
until someone decides to go home–
next week it begins all over again
enriching their busy retirement lives

7

death with sugar

old men are
loved by grandkids,
tell silly stories,
in funny voices,
adored by family

they are so kind,
sweet as sugar,
then go to congress
to send others'
children off to war,
with slogans, thoughts, and prayers
guns and tanks

afterward,
they return home
to play sweetly with
their grandchildren again

voting

harsh halogen light
from the gymnasium ceiling
casts shadows
on the basketball court
where voting machines wait

lines of people
stand inside, expecting to vote,
folded sample ballots
held in clenched hands
as poll watchers,
retired seniors earning a few bucks,
stand to the side observing

after hours of waiting,
like a rottweiler biting down
on fresh meat,
the lever is pressed,
determined to get the incumbent out,
a vote is cast–
tallies will be made,
the election over,
a winner decided

nobody takes up arms
if their chosen person
doesn't win, or declare
an unjust election–
they go home peacefully
except for right-wing fascists
masquerading as republicans
trying to overturn an election

heartache

he sits in his chair watching news,
yet hears nothing; his mind wanders
to yesterday, he overheard his son
say his father's emails are labeled spam

it meant nothing to the son
he graduated college owing nothing,
lived rent-free in manhattan
while working his first job,
or money loaned when he bought his first home

heartbroken, since he always helped
people in need–
hired ex-convicts
who couldn't find a job,
loaned money to people in desperate need, interest-free,
sometimes never repaid it,
or reduced rent to zero on a family in dire straits

alone, the television drones on
to deaf ears
as the blanket of depression smothers out all sounds

his right-wing trump loving son
has a mutant genetic gene, he thinks to himself;
sadly,
he deletes the son's contact information
from his phone

america

july fourth is a reminder
america is a conglomerate,
of many,
from everywhere,
merged together
under a constitution
to form a more perfect union,
where everyone belongs,
not only self-anointed
racist white nationalists

five minutes

i knew him all my life,
supported me,
paid for my education,
though we never said
we loved each other

a father-son relationship
can be very deep,
yet shallow,
both at the same time
until the end
comes unexpectedly

the nurse told me
before i entered
his ICU cubical
i can have five minutes
before he goes
into emergency surgery–
what do you say
in so little time
that was never
said in a lifetime?

slice

after eating, she sits in her room
alone
thinking of the day just past
depressed
no place to go tonight
no one to be with

years ago
this isn't how she thought
her life
would be growing up–
at thirty-five, not with anyone

the knife in her hand
gently
slices across,
pain
releases fleeting endorphins,
blood oozes down
                    her
                      arm to the table
maybe she'll call someone
to talk to, maybe not–
she listens
to young children
play below her window,
running. laughing, giggling

tomorrow is another day
another
body part,
another reason
to hold the blade

two-faced

republican governors
are against
mandating mandates
for masks and vaccines,
they strongly believe
in personal liberties

yet they are okay with
mandating against a
woman's individual
right to choose
regarding her body,
regarding abortion

texas politicians voted
a woman has no rights
or personal liberties
concerning her body

summer in vermont 1957

a large truck came to pick up
my steamer trunk
filled with camp clothes
to ship to vermont–
soon to be followed
by me at pennsylvania station,
gently shoved on a train
as my parents waved goodbye–
they smiled as i looked out the window
wondering
if i will ever see them again

camp deerfield
was not what i'd call a luxury camp,
rustic would be a compliment–
swim time was in a lake
teeming with fish, snakes, frogs, and salamanders
where some of my nazi bunkmates
tore legs off of them
waiting to see if they grew back

archery sucked
until one kid asked another
to pick up arrows,
then took aim–
both were sent home,
one in an ambulance–
rifle practice was incredible,
as i imagined
my neighborhood bully
standing in front of the target;
i thought of it as inner-city training

then there were the never-ending
bataan death marches in the mountains
for bus riding inner-city youth, where we
walked on abandoned train tracks (they told us)
until my legs started to vibrate;
some boys placed pennies on the iron rails
hoping to flatten them
while i slid down the embankment
on my rear end as the locomotive
passed inches above

it was there i met carmel,
a redhead from somewhere in massachusetts–
both being twelve,
it was a wonderful exploratory summer–
being young and naive, i
never took her home address,
never saw her again
except in my dreams; although
we had a loving life together
on many nights after

zoom poetry group metaphors

can you put it up for me, she asked

     i would love to, he replied
     have to open something first
     before i can bring it up,
        can you see it now?

yes, but it looks small,
can you make it bigger?

     not a problem, i need to play with it a bit
     he said, *looking at her on the screen*
     what about now?

yes, much better, i like it,
very impressive

     great, can you feel it?

i'm trying, but i can't get my head around it

     oh, sorry. i really wanted it to touch you

that's okay, sometimes i'm just not in the
mood, things have to grow on me
to appreciate them

     i understand; maybe next time
     we come together you can feel me

i look forward to it; in the past, you always
satisfied my passions

new car

he worked years, long hours,
many overtimes, no vacation,
to save for a car
to drive to work

finally had enough,
the used car dealer
smiled when he took the cash
and handed over the keys

after he twists the ignition,
puts it in drive,
then makes a right turn to leave–
doesn't see the stolen car
speeding toward him

splat

the last unicorn in manhattan

the bar is not hectic
as she sits by herself
at the far end, nursing a drink
to celebrate her birthday

another year another beer
friends come, friends go
none stick around; by herself
for another calendar event

fun times are in the past
as is her beauty–
facial lines abound,
toned muscles now relax,
sag where once taut;
a rounded beer belly
stretches her waist

if only she said yes
life might be better now–
offers to a sexual unicorn
were numerous, she slept with couples,
commitment scared her,
not many like her are around–
too late to attract the glitter crowd
she once romped with, she thought;
as the half-filled glass is raised, then emptied–
holding on to the bar
she stumbles out the door
to go home   alone

occupied

the demons in the room
are stuck inside with me,
they roam in my mind
then leave
    only to return
when i hear the world
outside
living life

they talk to me,
things i want to forget
or don't understand,
the whiskey chases them away—
it stopped working long ago,
leaving them stuck with me,
trapped in my inner thoughts

virus

the lawns in the neighborhood
were turning brown
from an airborne fungus,
until lawn services
offered to spray them free

almost everyone
took advantage,
except for those
who believed
their lawn seeds superior,
will repel disease,
won't die

they were wrong,
their lawns shriveled
   then
      died
like the unvaccinated will

man on lawn

going home
from a doctor appointment
i drove past a house
surrounded by forest–
saw a man
with a day's growth of beard
sitting on the front lawn,
under a bunch of tall trees,
on a burnt umber colored chair
rusted from the elements,
never painted

he is staring out
expressionless
looking at cars
that whiz past,
wearing a blue tee shirt
with a small chest pocket,
khaki-colored pants,
on a wednesday
at ten in the morning–
i thought, why isn't he working

he is sitting still,
breathing, i think,
maybe he should see my doctor?

if he is still there tomorrow
i'll call an ambulance–
hope he shaves,
then i'll know he got up

zoom poetry group

the white-haired lady
has a name, except
the zoom screen so small,
my eyesight so blurry,
cataracts so present–

i need to wait for someone
to say her name
before i can send her
a private chat

her poem
is about six ex-husbands,
seven ex-lovers,
her current sexual void,
her current biological needs

young nubile girls
are not for me,
at seventy-five
i'm not ready for heaven,
although
i think it really depends
on how one gets there

a beautiful patch of lawn

in the middle of brooklyn
there once was a patch
of luxurious, thick grass—
when klieg lights turn on
they shone down on the field,
the close-cut stalks shimmered with the wind

ebbets field is a mecca of baseball,
a source of pride
to the denizens of "wait till next year" fame
who never give up hope of a world series win—
emmet kelly, in costume, romps on the infield
to the crowd's delight while they waited
for the bums to leave the dugout

in 1955, euphoria
they win
their first world series—
people yell, car horns honk,
sirens blare, joyous mayhem;
years of wishes and prayers fulfilled

divorce is not pleasant—
hatred spews out when
lovers are spurned—
hearts broken,
the bums left; they
moved to tinsel town,
millions of crushed souls
in their wake

carbs and calories

as they walk through the cookie aisle
he reaches out, grabs a box of chocolate cookies

no, put it back, too many carbs and calories, she says
　　they walk some more

he reaches out, grabs a box of fudge-covered graham
crackers

no, put it back, too many carbs and calories
　　they walk some more

he reaches out, grabs a box of chocolate donuts

no, put it back, too many carbs and calories
　　they walk some more

you need to find a low carb, low-calorie substitute
to grab when you want something to satisfy your urges,

NO! not here, and not now!

endings

the darkness approaches
without notice
ending the sunlight—
she sits at the kitchen table,
her heart
beats
uncontrollably,
unrestrained

one handful
holds the relief she seeks,
small round pills;
hesitant
for the moment,
while the other
fingers
a glass of water

a tabby
leaps onto a familiar lap
curls in a ball,
ready for a comforting hand–
it looks up,
waits,
waits for gentle backstrokes

a phone rings
again,
again,
again
                 unanswered

heat

as the sun sets
a red summer moon
glows
in the preamble to darkness
while my eyes lock on
the evening sky–
folklore says
a burning moon
portends a hot,
humid day ahead–
i shower to cool off,
turn on the fan
so my date for the evening
will be comfortable
when she arrives–
the bedroom will soon
feel like tomorrow,
unbearable heat, and moist,
filled with sweating bodies
bringing the weather inside
until she leaves an hour later–
then i will sit
by the open window
alone,
looking up to the stars again

gameshow

can you guess
    how much it cost?
can you decide
    which door to pick?
will you step up
    to play the game of love
when most will
    probably choose wrong?

we decide on lovers
    by superficial things
what is needed
    to keep a couple together?
who knows?
    love is really a game show

school lunch

get in line,
stand one after the other,
the school cafeteria
serves hot lunch
on a cold plate
placed on a warm metal tray
to carry across the room
to a big tin garbage pail
so you can have desert
without a teacher asking
why
as you dump the mess
called nutritious food
where it belongs

the government proclaims
tomato ketchup is a vegetable–
you learn early in life
money talks,
kids don't matter,
politicians get greased,
farmers get paid,
poor kids stay poor,
hunger permanent
education secondary,
paying for votes in congress
number one

momma

i'm old now
over the hill
i feel so alone
without you here
i miss you so much

i want to talk
hold your hand
like we did
years ago
when you walked me
to bed at night

we talked about problems
we talked about good times
we talked about everything
who can i talk to now
i'm facing the end soon

thinking inward

the pinwheel on my lawn
spins freely with the breeze,
goes faster with a strong gust
or stops with a stillness

in my youth, the wind was at my back
blowing me forward into life–
my lance at the ready, charging ahead
without a care in the world, surging

i lost a few battles, won some too–
my trophies, looking back, are many:
humility, wisdom, empathy, and love
for others who try to make a go of life

a room in your home

the kitchen is the furnace of the home
where the heat of a family
is cooked over a table
where everyone sits to eat
then discuss the day's events or problems

school applications are filled out
as are team forms to join or travel,
homework drudgery is done there too,
as are the days mail for bills,
checks are written to pay them–
letters from loved ones
too far away are cried over
or bring smiles to a face

it's in this room
you decide to accept marriage,
or break an engagement,
to ask for advice, or not–
people will enter and leave your life,
yet the kitchen will never change;
you will remember every inch,
every floor tile, wallpaper, or paint,
forever burnished in your memory

vaccine choice

the sheep
keep going forward
they follow
the one in front
through a fence door
down the ramp,
past the exit
ignoring it,
into the
slaughterhouse
where death awaits

just before the butcher
slices into their throat
they think back to the exit–
the cleaver shouts out
"too late, you missed your chance"

the beach

waves roll in

lap at her legs

while she stands frozen

in the surf

eyes straight ahead–

sailboats float by in the distance

a hot summer sun beats down

a colorful beach umbrella offers shade

beckoning those who seek relief
to sit, relax, then look at the blue ocean

i watch her walk in the water
until she disappears from sight

forever

oreos

she always takes out six–
stacks the circular disks
in front of a glass
filled almost to the top
with ice-cold milk
stored in the rear of the fridge

with a forefinger and thumb
she lifts the top one,
then dunks it repeatedly
until the cookie almost falls apart

carefully placed on her tongue
savors the now soft chocolate wafer–
it releases sandwiched white sugar
as it smothers her tongue,
exploding sweetness sends
endorphins dancing in the brain

after each one, milk washes it down

the stack is gone, the glass empty,
she reaches for the package
still filled with rows of temptation–
the milk container has nothing left

ma, we need more milk!

dinner

standing at the stove
adjusting the flames
she tends the food
in the front, tall pot

stirs the contents
mixes it up
they all should warm
not burn or brown

finally plated
served while still hot
franks and beans
i can eat a lot

scaffolding

manhattan
is a jumble of chaos
from river to river,
nothing moves,
cars bumper to bumper
go in unison from
traffic light to traffic light
while pedestrians walk between

on the sidelines
are buildings
so tall you can't see
where they end–
always under construction,
shielded from sight
by large black nets
to catch fallen bricks and mortar,
landing on thick wooden planks
lying over sidewalks

lawyers
are the scaffolding of society;
occasionally blackhearted,
needed at times,
sometimes ugly
yet they hold society
together, under law,
amidst the falling debris in life

anti-vaccine names

they are americans who value their
independence who refuse to get
the shot, their choice, a right
they say, like the flu, no worse

these are the names
they should go by–
brain dead,
soon-to-be-dead,
a person waiting to die,,
a person who can infect others,
a f'n stupid person
is the final one

modern medicine

i knew my maternal grandmother
loved me, she still lives on in memory,
but one grandmother is missing
from my vision–
she died fifteen years
before i arrived

i never heard her voice
or felt her gentle touch,
missed her arms of love
to envelop me with passion
only heard tales from dad about her

she died from disease that now can be cured
as i'm sure others dying now
will one day in the future be saved
if they can hold on long enough–
the reason they die is because of money

do we need wars, killing machines,
instead of research facilities,
paying for education so doctors
can be brought online, lives saved,
families enjoying life together
instead of at funerals

reading primer fantasy

see the white picket fence
see Spot run
run Spot run
run to the house
Dick looks at Spot
Jane opens the door
come in, Dick, Sally is here
Dick kisses Jane,
kiss Jane kiss
Sally kisses Dick
kiss Dick, kiss
Jane kisses Sally
Dicks hands roam
all over Sally
Jane slips some tongue
Sally wants some too
Dick, Jane, and Sally
all go to bed together
Spot waits outside

months later
Jane has a baby
Sally does not have a baby
because Dick had a vasectomy
Jane is easy

time

there is no time in yesterday
it is gone, can't be brought back,
as well as time for tomorrow;
it doesn't exist until then

time is only now,
fleeting,
comes and goes
just as quickly

time is in the moment,
doesn't last long,
really can't even measure it

holding hands,
kisses linger,
remembered love is like time,
it's a moment to treasure
gone too soon

the man in the garage

he was old, very old, hunched over
he sits in a wheelchair,
with his garage door open
a blank stare on his face
i wonder what his life was like
as a young man

on afternoon walks
i wave to him,
never receive one back
day after day   no response

his home aide
always smiles back
she'd sit next to him
in the garage, if she wasn't
walking miles to the market
to shop for food

one day the garage door didn't open
the aid was never seen again
a realtor's lockbox appeared on the front door

i wonder what his life was like
as a young man, everyone has a story,
some better than others–
death buries a body along with its history

steakhouse

steak, garlic, the dark walnut stained
walls appear masculine, as they sit,
look at the menu to make a selection;
prime rib, porterhouse, or sirloin
all dry-aged, cooked to near perfection

rare, medium, or well done ruined,
ketchup must be requested as
it's removed after each meal–
extra-sharp knives placed on the table

the low drone of conversation
floats in the air, broken by the sound
of sizzling steak served from the right,
while the aroma wafts upward,
scorches the senses

saliva puddles in the mouth,
scoops of butter melt in a split,
salted baked potato–
no one speaks, ecstasy starts,
the orgasmic meal has begun

a 21-ounce ice cold beer
on tap is served; it cleanses the palette–
he sits back when finished,
one life experience at a time savored, he thinks,
the next one when he brings her home

old men

old men don't have to shave every day
    why should they?
no one visits during the week
they eat breakfast in pj's
    may get dressed
    so they can sit all-day
    to watch television

if it's not too hot or cold
they'll go outside for a walk
hope they don't trip or fall
with no one to help them up
    then pray they remember
    how to get back home

of course, there's always the chair
in the backyard where one can watch
the clouds float past
    or the hawk that flies overhead
    then attacks a starling midair
    for its dinner

like yankee stadium

bottom of the ninth
last game of the season
score is tied
the home team at bat

first batter up
is a power hitter,
waits out two pitches
    looks at the ball,
swings and misses–
next pitch hits
to left field,
he's now on first base

the second batter up
takes a practice swing or two
warming up,
the infield backs up,
the pitcher throws a fastball,
it zooms toward home–
a perfect bunt
down the third base line,
runners on first and second

third batter uses the bat
to knock dirt off his cleats–
the pitch is a curveball,
he hits it to center field,
high and far, it gets lost in the sun,
bases are loaded–
the crowd is electrified

morton feinberg always bats in the ninth,
everyone must get one at-bat,
it's a league rule–
at twelve, he's the youngest
and smallest player in the game

adjusts his glasses, scrawny legs shake,
fingers wrap around the wooden bat
waiting for his first hit of the season

he knows the game is on his shoulders
the pitcher winds up
a hardball whizzes at him,
        hits his left shoulder

morty walks to first,
the kid on third comes home,
feinberg won the game
and the world series   in his mind–
everyone rushes him
        they all walk home later
        for milk and cookies

perilous times 2021

the sun is out today
dark clouds of sedition
are in the past, i hope

time will tell
if an oath
to the constitution
has more value
than blind loyalty
to an individual

one civil war
is enough
no need
for more to die

measurements

he sent cupid's arrow
flying to her heart
but missed by a smidge-
the tail feathers left a smudge of love
just enough to get noticed, yet
there is not a schtickle of amore
to mean something–
he was hoping for a speck of romance,
not the slightest scrap of interest is shown–
dejected
he puts away a fistful of arrows
hoping for better aim next time

untitled

there once were three wise men in Chelm
whose intellect would surely overwhelm
the most brilliant men in the realm
a rowboat they could not even helm

if one were to ask their advice
you'd need to ask it twice
although they are very nice
their answers are like playing dice

similarities

software programs are like husbands
occasionally they work properly
other times they screw up royally
plus, they are always there to yell at

it all has to do with settings–
before you start with either
make sure the rules are firmed up
don't rush or overlook something

it is tough to reprogram both

moving out

she watches
as the moving truck pulls away–
the house is empty, its contents gone

downsizing,
nothing left inside
except for memories
of when
  she brought her first child home
  a daughter showed an engagement ring
  the letter her husband was promoted
  mom moved in after dad died

numerous birthdays
family gatherings
the sad days too

the house is made of just wood and wires–

the tears on her cheek are filled with memories

searching

when deer hunting season starts
the stags with large antlers
are sought after
   end up stuffed
   hung in someone's bar

does are left
for the other hunters
to seek out, shoot,
   suspended on a wall
   over a television

alone, the deer are
missing their mate
in the forest,
searching for food
and others like them

not unlike humans
when a lover dies
people are lonely,
missing companionship

they search for new love–
not to replace,
   but to begin anew

carol's cat

on padded paws, it slithers
across the video screen
a shadow against the bright light
from the sunny window behind

like a mirage, it appears
then is gone, never still,
nameless, i never hear
her call it, yet it exists

like all felines, a mystery,
keeping to itself,
guarding the home
against small intruders

seeds

seniors like to place flowers
in the front of their home,
small ceramic pots overflowing
with color to brighten a green lawn

in the retirement village
grandchildren often visit
to help their grandmother
plant seeds, then water them

five-year-old mollie put seeds
she found at school in a small
metal bucket, behind the tall tree
in the middle of the front yard

the seeds grew, taller and taller–
no one noticed due to aging eyesight
and cataracts, till police rang one day–
seems mollie is growing marijuana
in her bucket on grandma's front lawn

beach in july

the ocean water's cold today
as i stand waist-deep from land–
rough seas, i think are coming,
waves tumble, it's hard to stand

a strong white crest unexpectedly
comes from behind to knock me down
bumping into an unseen beauty;
i thought maybe she would drown

some say its love at first sight,
a face so fine and fragile
i found an earthbound angle–
my pulse beats with delight

oh, the life i want to have with her
a home filled with joy all-day
but alas it was not to be, i found,
as mermaids tend to swim away

poetic romance

they make a good couplet
his word flow is melodic
she likes the way he said syllables
especially his last quatrain

she especially loves to rhyme
he didn't want to waste time
but she played him like a mime
until the ring cost a pretty dime

grandma

she entered a marriage of necessity
not one of love
the person i adored
overflowed with it

a mother's deathbed request
see my children marry jewish–
after death
bessie, etta, and frances
lived with an aunt,
julian, the brother, went to an orphanage

a stranger brought grandma to america
to marry, *only if my siblings come too–*
once here, he reneged to bring them

his friend said he would do it–
that man became my grandfather,
emotionally shallow, with
cold business instincts–
he kept his word,

she tried to keep her promise to her mother

sat shiva when the baby sister
eloped with a non-jew

never knew the sister existed till i was past forty–
i healed the rift after ninety years had passed

ring on the finger

his eyes are frozen
a steady gaze on her,
they see nothing else
but soft features

lips he cherishes to kiss
arms yearn to embrace
to hold her tight–
she emanates sweetness
female hormones
float in the air

he cannot approach
or cross the red line–
he dares not
for fear she will think
less of him

hopelessly
he realizes
it may never be;
yet he thinks someday,
maybe,   someday

postman

i saw the postman today–
he looks pale, with dark
circles under his eyes,
not like years ago
when he skipped up the front steps
to slip mail through the slot,
then trudge
house to house,
street to street,
mile after mile
carrying a heavy leather bag
on his shoulder filled with letters–
he was younger then,
looked healthy, not like today
where he drives a truck
house to house
to open a mailbox door
without stepping out–
the first time i met him
he had me sign
a receipt for divorce papers–
he stood waiting, said nothing,
i think he knew–
now, years later
we both aged,
we both walk slower,
we both look like old men
no longer skipping,
no longer looking
    for the next letter

to s.v. (in response to her breakup poem)

if i was not a married man,
and you were not a lesbian,
oh, the poetry we could write
while limbs were deeply entangled

romeo and juliet are but an afterthought
cyrano and his beloved only a whisper
jay gatsby and daisy buchanan a fleeting memory
we are hotter than a summer sun at noon

alas, the world isn't how we want it–
love doesn't always float in our direction
while bumps and pitfalls we must endure
from the wretched people who come along

someday cupid may stumble near
to shoot unstraight arrows into open arms–
the secret is to keep an unlocked heart,
to listen for the wisps of love

numbers

nineteen
forty-one
fifty-four
sixty-five

we all hit different numbers
as our age keeps adding up
hopefully, we reach the high ones
although some never will

live life for today
laugh, make memories
love like you never did before
you only get one shot this time around

critics and readers

i never understood
some of their poems–
they use multi-syllabic
twenty dollar words
with meanings only
a well versed
english major would know,
it drives me
to a dictionary,
or to the next poem

one group of poets
near an ivy league college
are excellent writers,
when you have a degree
in interpreting poetry,
have deep esoteric knowledge,
or enjoy being talked down to

i prefer to be a reader
on a chair under a tree
reading of someone's life or loves
plain speak, if you will;
it's so much more enjoyable–
maybe then
more people would buy poetry books

7/11

he stands
behind the counter
with his dark skin,
deep asian accent,
speaks softly,
politely,
as he was brought up to do

not here long enough
to have an american attitude;
that will change soon enough,
as the son of a bitch
standing in front of him
with a gun
demands the results
of his ten-hour shift,
of his standing,
of his lifting,
of his stacking boxes
to support a wife and newborn child
only to lose it,
as the result
of america's second amendment,

the pool

the hot summer sun
beats down
as the chilly cold water
refreshes my spirit

i swim under the surface
to cool off,
then lay on a float
in calm, still water

after a while, ripples appear,
the water gets choppy, rough,
noise out of nowhere shatters silence,
the water isn't so cold anymore

the pool is filled with kids
they jump in, splash, yell,
the water is now much warmer–
too many little pishers playing in it

silence

when people are deaf
they use sign language
or read lips
to understand
what others are saying,
or watch subtitles on the news
to keep in touch
with life's activities

i am at a loss
why 70 million people
who claim to be patriots,
are supporters of law and order
saw,
heard, or
read about
an insurrection
instigated
by the president
of the united states

are mute

after a near coup
was almost successful

wrong decision

nurses walk into her room
dressed in hazmat suits,
they don't want to catch the virus–
at forty-two, she finally has her act together
but made a decisioin to refuse
a vaccine due to articles
she read online

now she is fighting to live

a mother of two kids,
she struggled with addiction issues
    but overcame them,
started life anew
when she turned thirty-eight,

her parents are distraught;
this did not have to happen,
what is to become of her
children if she dies,
decisions need to be made

the doctor turns off the ventilator,
tubes are withdrawn
decisions need to be made

the card store

every time i need to send a card
the selection is overwhelming

when i read the message written inside,
they all seem the same

they remind me of your kisses,
our arms embraced, holding tight

a powerful summer romance
so short and sweet remembered

just like the cards i read

warehouse for men

on a wooded country road
in the middle of rural nowhere
i pass the state home for men
with low slung weathered buildings
in need of paint and repair

unshaven gentlemen
wander aimlessly around
or sit on folding chairs
under tall trees on unmowed lawns

dressed in soiled white tee shirts
while others wear dollar store clothes
with baggy slacks or rumpled jeans
they sit and smoke all-day

most need a haircut–
they wander about
with a seeming distant stare
if not seated on a bench or chair

a deer stands on the roadside
as i drive by the old men's home,
it watches me   as i watch the men,
who watch no one   as their life passes by

unseen

the homes are all
neat and tidy,
lined up
row after row,
block after block,
manicured lawns all,
a look of outward respectability

the widow alone
in a dark kitchen
every night, with one to talk to,
is unseen

the wife whose husband left
for another warm body to love,
is desperate to find work,
tries to figure out her life,
is unseen

a husband sleeps on the floor
after passing out from liquor
while his wife puts a cold compress
on sore, beaten cheeks,
is unseen

the teenager at night
in an upstairs bedroom
snorts drugs to get high,
parents downstairs
are unseen

life is not what it appears to be

barbie doll does the beach

she left the gym
before noon
after she packs
her melons
in a tight crop top

the weights on the floor
only toned her upper body
while her mushy tushy
was swaying with every step,
attracting glares and stares
from everyone she walks past

in her parked car
by the nude beach
she undresses,
then prances onto the sand
with a beach blanket and lotion
to get an allover natural tan,
where she is noticed by all

gay men wanted to be her,
lesbians wanted to be with her,
straight single men were intimidated by her,
married men wanted to sleep with her

the truth of the matter
is only her doctor knows,
what you see
is not how she began,
in more ways than one

menage a trois

is french for two plus one is three

is french for playing well with others

is french for monogamy is dead

is french for where was i years ago

the fearless bar and lounge

a petite woman
wears a dark blue tank top
with the skinniest arms, i ever remember seeing,
a red tattoo in a foreign language on her forearm,
then sits on the stool next to me, turns slightly,
and smiles at me with an alluring smirk

"how 'bout buying a girl a drink"
as the jukebox started to play an elvis tune
while the band set up for tonight's live show–
"sure, what'll you have"

"whatever you drink at home is fine with me"

the backpack she wore that night
had all her worldly possessions–
two years later, she kissed me good morning
then went out for her daily walk, her backpack
only slightly fuller and did not return

i never found out
where she went,
or came from,
i don't think it's important–
i found what i thought was love,
at least for a while;
maybe someday
she'll walk back into my life

maybe

second place

i reach in between,
thought i found paradise,
later we finish the whiskey

in the morning
i woke up,
realized
the beauty queen
i brought home last night
only competed,
never won

but why should my luck change

ecstasy

are your kisses on my lips,
each stroke of your hands
on my waiting figure,

is your tongue
as it glides over skin
then slithers
slowly
downward

i lose control of my body to
your will,
your love,
your embrace

exhausted
i arise each morning wanting more
but dreams are not real

carnival ride

when the carnival
comes to town
each year
i ride the slow-moving
tunnel of love

the same thing
every summer,
killer humidity,
no lights
no surprises,
no thrills,
no one to hold tight
since you left

payback

it was difficult
for her to do it,
jump-off
the bridge of home
with heartfelt faith
i would be there

the security blanket
she knew all her life
is left behind
for her to be with me

i did not disappoint

through illness,
sadness
smiles,
and laughter,
i only wanted
to be with her,
all the time,
including
at the end
when she paid me back
with
"i love you"
one last time

hockey arena

all the tier's eyes
ignore the puck
flying on the ice
as a small sparrow
flutters from high above
to sit near a penalty box
on the glass wall
above two players
who throw down gloves
to exchange punches
while the referee stands frozen
watching
the small unticketed fan

harry the ice cream man

never knew what was in the freezer
on his truck, besides ice cream,
sometimes he sold fireworks to us
other times he had other stuff to sell

all the kids knew him since grade school–
he would go fishing with my friend's dad
and his buddy on weekends, who was a
writer for various fishing magazines

in winter, he'd stand in front of a local school
selling hot potato knishes, hawking them
to the kids as they walk out after class–
eventually, he was gone;   he melted away

teeth marks

were indented
on the yellow #2 pencil
when she handed it to me

i felt queasy
holding it
between my fingers
knowing her saliva
coated it,
while her tongue
ran along its sides

i look back on that day
many decades later,
what was i thinking

after school let out
almost every afternoon
we experimented as lovers
through junior high school

after college
she married my cousin–
i never told him
she worked as a sugar baby
to pay for her tuition

somethings
are best left unsaid, i guess,
since the college president
changed all her grades

broccoli

a green veggie
side dish
not especially good looking,
plus it smells
once cooked,
stinks up the place

i pour the water
that cooked it,
down the drain,
Its nutrients boiled out

this reminds me of
what you did to our love

revision

oh no,
did i write that tripe?
why was there a comma
instead of a hyphen,
what was i thinking

a poet writes,
can rewrite
ten or twenty
or fifty times;
like a painter
who never finishes,
always touches up
      here or there
the paintbrush
rarely dries out
until his muse
walks away
to get dressed

reality

how do you talk
   to people who don't listen
how do you reason with people
   who don't want to understand

science is based on facts
   one plus one equals two
faith is based on beliefs
   one plus one is three

you can't change
a faith-based
person's beliefs

faith is not based on facts

brewmasters

on an inner-city street
a man bought a building
then filled it with stills,
hired brewers,
purchased hops
to mix with the yeast,
overcame the cooking stench
to make an amber fluid–
finally out came
the drink he desired

this is his brew

trump said it's not fair,
a stolen election–
called for the crowds 'cause
his cronies didn't vote it down,
they stormed the capital's steep steps
then massed in small halls
created a stench that shook
the nation's foundation–

his revolution failed
against
the constitution he swore
to defend

this is his brew

sitting for hours

the doorbell rings
enrages my dog,
barking starts
i open the door–
in walks my company
friends for years,
we sit at the table
to eat then gab
and gab
and gab
and gab

my tush starts to hurt

why can't we move
to more comfortable
seats

no one asks,
no one stirs,
soon they'll leave
the pain will pass
pass the cake
the coffee too

new york subway

she sat next to me
on the train to work,
a smile
on a nasty winter day
warms the trip,
it's not so cold then

we spoke of nothing,
yet it felt important

there was magic
in the moment

fleeting,
     gone
when her stop came along;
we never met again

keys of death

composers are inspired
by life, writing music
to reflects events
of society

war has piano keys
pounding to the battle,
while a melody
of lost love
lilts along

music
moves us emotionally
as our soul hears the tunes,
but something has to die
for the ivory keys
to reach our heart

forbidden love

it is crystal clear–
we see each other unhampered,
often talk about many things
yet we do not dare speak of love

the glass wall is in front of us
we cannot touch it, invisible,
we both know it's there,
erected by society, mentally sustained

we are untouchables, so close,
yet denied a tender caress,
restricted to monogamy
in an era of free love and polyamory

if glass walls shatter,
sharp shards fall on us,
injuring reputations, marriages,
bank accounts and children

oh, so many

kindness and love
is all he requires,
learning disabled
help is needed

meanness does not exist
in his simple mind,
god, or nature,
made him so

he is part of
someone's family,
loved and adored,
a child to be cherished

the present

she was sixteen
i was seventeen
rural hopatcong
was where it happened

the moon was covered
clouds forecast a rainy day;
a transistor radio was on,
it plays love songs of the year

we found a clearing
in the woods, off a back
road somewhere dark,
isolated, late at night

her treasure was gifted,
a once in a lifetime event,
vows of forever love made,
it was a summer romance

i never forgot her name
or a wonderful youthful night–
evenings alone i think of her often;
today i found her obit online,

ode to desire

from my mind's mist
she appears to float,
her every step is magic
through a field of flowers,
    with bare feet
      pebbles turn to dust

as she slowly swirls past
the tightly wound buds,
they open to bloom,
their fragrance sweet

hardened hearts melt,
only kindness
blossoms in her presence,
love descends
to touch everyone

the love of my heart
    walks there;
if only my secret's desire
    was aware of my feelings;
but it will never be
    in this lifetime;
maybe the next one

revolution #3

armed bolsheviks race to the palace–
the czar's personal guards
defend with deadly force,
but they are overrun–
the royal household fell,
kidnapped, killed, and buried,
the revolution is a success,

militants run up the steps,
right-wing nationalists proud
to call themselves patriots
race into the halls of congress
intent to hang their vice president,
shoot the speaker of the house–
they fail to overturn democracy
based on a constitution, many
took an oath to defend

police did not use deadly force
when hundreds overturned barricades,
put their feet on the first steps
of the nation's capital, then
sacked, looted, and defecated
in the halls of government

revolutionaries gamble
with their life,
some win, some lose,
on january 6th
                    we all lost something

if only they were sick today

what do you say
when you think back
to your father
telling you
    his mother died
at forty-two
from a cancer
today is curable

on tonight's news
it reported a man
received
a heart transplant
infected with hepatitis C,
which today has a cure;
i think back
    to my mother
who died
not that many years ago
from the same infection

if only they were sick today

the summer bus

after summer class at nyu
i went to the port authority terminal
in midtown manhattan
to ride the lakeland bus
to landing, new jersey

as it turned and twisted down a concrete ramp
the bus wormed its way into the lincoln tunnel–
i was amazed at the intricate simplicity
of how they built it
in the middle of manhattan

the bus stops along the way in boonton,
a historically old town built on a mountain
with narrow bending streets;
it is amazing to me how
the bus navigated through

the homes are all pre World War One vintage-
i imagine seeing dick and jane
skip by the short white picket fences
with spot yapping at their heels,
as they did in my elementary primer

finally, the bus stops by the train station
at lake hopatcong– i step off the bus
then wait for this week's girlfriend
to pick me up
to continue my summer fun

insecticide

red soldier ants race down tunnels
to tell the yellow-skinned queen of danger–
the adjacent field is using insecticide
to kill plant-eating ants

they urge precautions, dig deeper,
block all entrances;
but she ignores the warnings,
after all, she is safe and well-fed

her mother built many
ant colonies in this field,
she felt unharmed and secure–
if the worker ants stopped foraging
to dig deeper, she would be hungry

day after day, the poison came,
ant after ant fell ill then died–
after 700,000 red ants are dead,
the queen fell sick too

finally, she decides the colony
needs to dig deeper, take precautions,
but many don't; they believe what the queen
previously said, "it would disappear
in summer's heat," but they still died

half the worker ants left her colony
to join the blue ants in the other field,
secure their safety will be taken care of;
while the yellow-skinned queen gorges herself
alone in her chamber, her workers gone
long live the blue ant queen

irwin

he lived a full life,
married twice with two daughters
retired once, then started again
with a telephone company
high up in the world trade center

he was a caring person,
some would say a stand-up guy–
there was nothing he would not do
if he thought of you as a buddy

a work friend had a heart condition,
he could hardly walk a few feet–
on september 11
irwin took the day off
his friend went to work as usual

after the towers fell, the deaths numbered,
irwin was distraught his friend
died alone without him there,
he would have stayed with him till the end,
never leaving to save himself

family dinner

it's late at night
the brisket is cooking
onion and garlic attack
my senses while i strain
to restrain my saliva
as i anticipate tomorrow
when family comes to dinner

the sweet potato pie,
topped with burnt marshmallow
is scooped up by everyone-
pass this, please,
pass that, please
conversation turns to manners
then silence,
as food is consumed

it's been a while
since all four kids are together
now adults with families,
two divorced,
yet in my eyes
they never grew up,
not seen as equals
although they start to treat me
as if i need help doing things–
to be honest
sometimes i do,
the child has become the parent

what's in a name

don't know why whiskey
is also spelled whisky
or called scotch
or bourbon
since it all tastes good
once you drink it–
they say it depends
on where it comes from–
i'm more concerned
with which glass its poured in

i prefer a single malt
distilled ten years or more,
maybe twenty if i can afford it

not a fan of mixed liquor
although
there's nothing wrong with it,
guess it's a personal thing,
or gifted to me

jackie comes to long island

she drapes her clothes
over a desk chair
before she showers with him—
the joy experienced
when he takes a hand towel
to dry her, slowly caressing
every mound, every crevice
with tender care

leaning in,
slowly sliding down,
tender feathery kisses
on her neck feel wonderful,
his hand placed behind
her head pulls into him
for electrifying lust

an emotional moment
with her married lover,
minutes really, she wishes
would last forever;
she knows in an hour they
need to check out of the hotel

her husband's at work
at a law firm, always reading,
a bland life with dull interests

these afternoon trysts are
lightning in a bottle to her—
thrills of sin stimulate her,
seeks more and more, becomes insatiable—
she decides shortly after marriage
to lead a lifestyle as in a jackie collins novel

goodbye 9-11

where did it go,
our unified nation
shocked
saddened
not a dry eye   anywhere
right and left together
all americans
all citizens
with sorrow   remember the day

yet the malice which
inspired a fatal day
gave birth years later
to our division–
hatred of others
external anger turned internal,
start a war, stop a war
left against right
faith against science
faith against nonbelievers
faith against female rights,
them against us,
stop the vote, you must vote, they can't vote
national chaos
insurrection

did they win   years later

fetish (noun - an object regarded with awe)

my eyes can't help look at
the hourglass shape
as it walks ahead of me
only a few steps away

her face is hidden
she looks straight ahead
not turning around to see me,
obsessed with her movement

perhaps i should stay back,
it could become awkward
if she saw me stare;
i only stepped out to get some air

after all, it's been five blocks
since i decided to follow
for some unknown urge
i could not control

she stops her stroll
to enter a dress shop,
then reality hit
when i look in

see my reflection
in the glass window—
whatever possessed me
to follow, i wonder to myself

memories of brooklyn

after decades away, drove past the house where i grew
up. the street looks familiar yet has changed. the thick,
tall tree in front is missing, its outstretched arm crossed
the road, made my father nervous it might fall on a car
or person during a storm, wonder when it was cut down

the front door is gone, the old green painted one
replaced by redwood, with a brass mail slot on the
lower third– the porch has new windows, kind of
modern looking though the house is a pre-world war
one victorian style

i remember the kitchen where mom would cook minute
steaks for ten minutes; i was skinny back then, couldn't
eat her food–
my grandfather bought her an upright freezer placed in
the corner, filled it with only knishes (all kinds from
mrs stahls knishes in brighton beach), so when
company came to visit him after he moved in with us,
there'd be something to feed them

my bedroom on the second floor was in the corner,
exposed on two sides to winter's frigid winds, ice
would form on my windows–
i never entertained there except once when my sister's
girlfriend from rye new york slept over. it was an
exciting evening before my parents woke up early

the attic had a small maids apartment, though we never
had one; guess the decades before us might have–
i used it for a casino until mom closed me down; if not
for her, i might own a las vegas one right now

Please check the author's website for
more poetry books.

www.CreativeFiction.net

on **Instagram**, his account,
always has daily poems.

elliot_m_rubin

www.ingramcontent.com/pod-product-compliance
Lightning Source LLC
Chambersburg PA
CBHW060430260626
47161CB00005B/1857